You Are Magic

By Tierra Allen

Illustrated by Eric Muchira

You Are Magic

Copyright © 2021 by Tierra Allen

Written by Tierra Allen, Illustrated by Eric Muchira

All rights reserved, including the right of reproduction in whole or in part in any form.

For information, please contact

byTierra LLC at:

Tierra@bytierra.com

First Edition

ISBN 978-1-7373870-9-1

This book was written for you. By a girl who has no children, but can't wait to one day be a mom. She can't wait because she already knows, before they're even born... that they are MAGIC. And so are YOU.

To Ray, Rosalind, Shannon, and the rest of my incredibly powerful and amazing support systems... THANK YOU for guiding me to believe in myself and to believe in MAGIC, always.

by Tierra LLC

FOREWARD

We have all experienced times where we've been made to feel like we don't belong because we're different or we feel that all that we are and where we come from isn't good enough. In those moments, all we need to hear is that we are good enough. That's called an affirmation. To have your worth described or something kind expressed and explained can make all the difference in the world. An explanation that unfortunately most of us have never heard about ourselves until much later in life, if at all.

My hope for this book is to help children have the tools to get through tough times as they learn and gain confidence in who they are, where they come from, and ultimately, who they want to be.

Tierra Allen

In a small town, on the corner of Allen Street there was a beautiful white house with a big blue door. This house was surrounded by flowers of all colors, like the rainbow. The family that lived here had a young boy. His name was Magic.

Magic's family was huge! Some were tall and some were small. Some had straight hair and some had curly hair. Some were very old and some were very young. Some were white and some were brown. The people in Magic's family came in all different shades.

Although they seemed different, they weren't. They were a family and they all loved each other very much.

Magic was a strong boy. He had dark brown curls that covered his big round head in the wildest way. His reddish-brown skin was so dazzling it looked like a shiny penny. He had big, light brown eyes that glittered in the sun. And the biggest smile anyone had ever seen. Magic was always smiling and laughing. And happy. That happiness he carried was love.

He walked around like a man on a mission to make the world a better place.

And he was only 5...

Every year in the month of August, Magic's entire family went on vacation together. Vacation this year was going to be extra special because once they got back from Martha's Vineyard, Magic would be starting his first day of school!

Up until now, his family members had been his only playmates. Now, he would meet his new classmates that would all be his age and he'd spend five days a week- surrounded by these new playmates. In typical Magic fashion, he couldn't be happier or more excited.

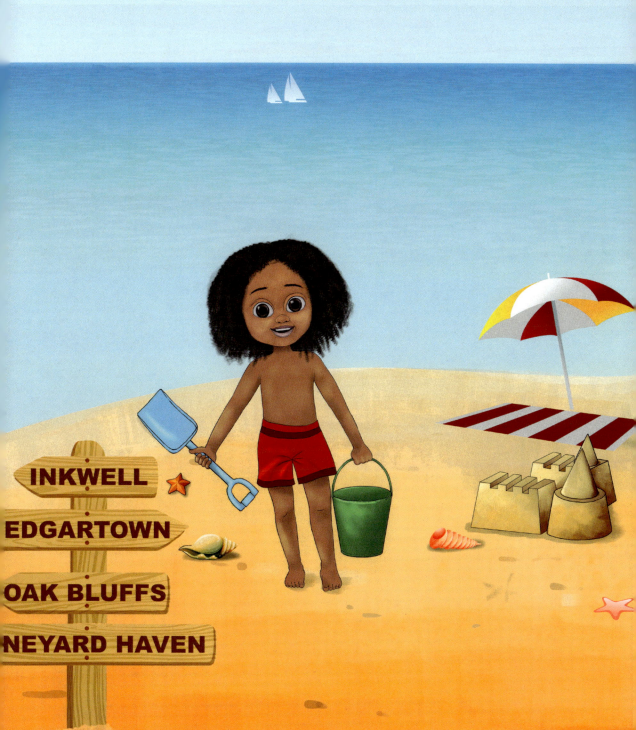

On the morning of the big day, Magic jumped out of bed before his alarm sounded. Full of excitement and energy, he brushed his teeth, and attempted to brush his smashed down curls. All with the biggest grin.

Once he finished his bowl of cereal, Magic put on his favorite blue tshirt and jean shorts and was off to the bus! With Js on his feet, HE was ready.

After anxiously waiting in line at his bus stop, Magic finally made it to his seat. As the bus pulled off, he waved hard out the window as the bus got ready to take him into his highly anticipated first day of school.

& away the bus went...

At 3:45 pm on the dot, the bus pulled back up to the familiar corner of Allen Street where the neighborhood parents were all waiting. Magic's parents and grandparents were there holding balloons and signs and were cheering and shouting in anticipation for him to get off the bus from his very first day. They just knew he'd match their energy with his own.

but.... they were wrong.

The once bright light and excitement that filled his eyes just a few hours earlier seemed to have dimmed. As he slowly walked off of the bus with his head down— he handed his backpack to his dad, turned to his mom, buried his face into her legs, and began to cry.

Rubbing his back and bending down to look her son in the eyes, Magic's mom asked him what happened..

He told her how the kids on the bus touched his hair the whole ride there and back.

How when he reached class, the teacher called names and everyone laughed when his name was said out loud.

And how he felt so alone and different all day because he was the only kid in the class who looked like him. He was the brownest boy in the room.

At that moment, his mother smiled. As she wiped away his tears, she said " My special boy, DON'T YOU KNOW WHO YOU ARE?!"

Look at your grandpa, she said pointing to her father. He's who you get your will to succeed and be the best from. People all over the world know him because of his hard work and talent. You have that in you.

And look at your grandma Shan! That's where you get your kind heart and ability to love everyone you meet.

Look at your nana RoRo! I've seen you protect your friends and family the same way she's protected her family and the same way she protects YOU!

And your uncles! You have the same wild curls as some of them. They're where you get your wild spirit and competitive nature. They love you.

Now look at mommy and daddy. You get your strong arms and giving nature from your father. The ways he helps and gives back to others without hesitation is all magic. But you get your creativity from mommy. You're so smart. You can do anything you put your brilliant mind to. You're the best of us both- all in one.

We named you Magic because your loving spirit, wild and crazy curls, your beautiful brown skin, that big bright smile, and those big, brown, eyes remind us of the Magic that was used to create you. Our family is in you.

We all made you, and we love you.

Never let anyone steal your joy. Always do your best. Always be yourself. Your family loves you just as you are. Make sure you love yourself too! Magic smiled his usual big, toothy grin and blushed. As he looked around at all his family members who had shown up for him, he saw something familiar. He saw himself. He could feel their magic. He knew if they had his back, he could do or be anything in the world.

And they all walked home together...

The next morning Magic asked his mom to put his curls into a bun to keep the kids from touching his hair. She told him she thought he should let them be free and he should simply say "please don't touch my hair" to anyone that tried. But, to help him have a better second day, she bunned them up as he wished.

While waiting in line to board the bus, one kid said, "Hey Magic, what happened to your super cool hair?". Magic looked over at his parents and then back at his classmate and said "I'll let them out, but please don't touch my curls without asking". The kid nodded back in agreement.

His parents rushed over and his mom removed his hair tie. As she shook his hair loose and watched the relief sweep across her big boy's face, she could see his confidence rushing in with it. She could see he now knew exactly who he was. His mom kissed him on the forehead

.... and his dad gave him a big high five and whispered loud enough for only Magic to hear...

"We told you. You are Brave. You are loved. And You are Magic."

This book is dedicated to my strongest angel in heaven. My grandmother, Edith Ramsey. She always made me feel like I was the greatest person she'd ever met. She always believed in me, listened to me, and supported me. That confidence helped me become the woman I am today. I miss her every day.

Photo by @aprilbellephotos

Made in the USA
Columbia, SC
15 January 2022